LOVE
HAPPINESS

A Special Gift

For:

From:

Date:

6309 Airport Freeway
Fort Worth, Texas 76117

ISBN: 1-57051-451-8

Printed in China

How Does Your Garden Grow?

Brownlow

A Little Book of Blessings

A Little Book of Love

A Little Cup of Tea

A Roof With a View

Baby's First Little Book

Baby Oh Baby

Beside Still Waters

Catch of the Day

Dear Daughter • Dear Teacher

Friends

For My Secret Pal

Grandmother

Grandmothers are for Loving

Happiness Is Homemade

How Does Your Garden Grow?

Mom, I Love You

My Sister, My Friend

Quiet Moments of Inspiration

Seasons of Friendship • Sisters

Tea Time Friends

They Call It Golf

RICH SOIL
DAISY

Life begins the day
you start a garden.

—Chinese Proverb—

The man who has planted
a garden feels that he has
done something for the good
of the whole world.

—Charles Dudley Warner—

With a garden there is hope.

—Grace Firth—

A good deed is never lost;
he who sows courtesy reaps
friendship, and he who plants
kindness gathers love.

—Saint Basil—

What sunshine is to flowers,
smiles are to humanity.

—Joseph Addison—

SEED MIX
GARDEN of PLENTY

The Lord will guide you
always; he will satisfy your
needs in a sun-scorched land
and will strengthen your
frame. You will be like a
well-watered garden,
like a spring whose
waters never fail.
—Isaiah 58:11—

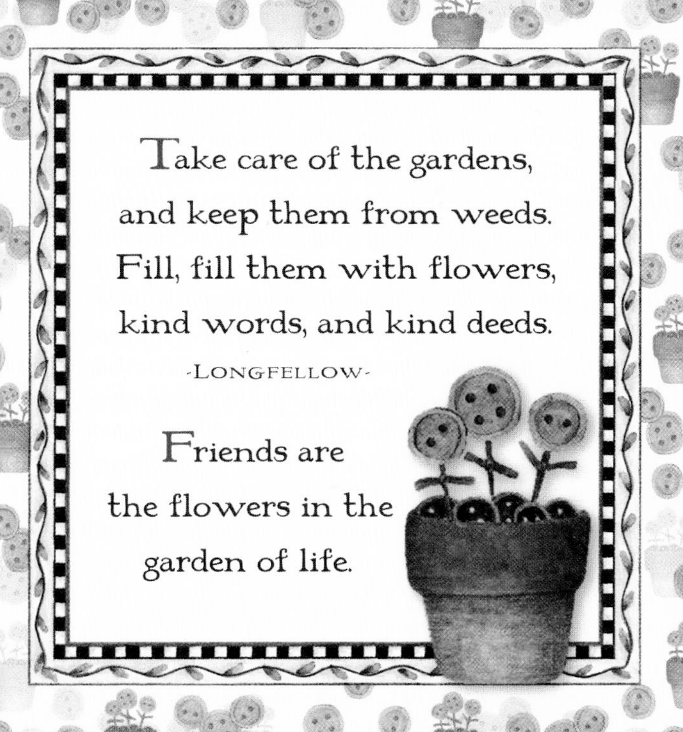
Take care of the gardens,
and keep them from weeds.
Fill, fill them with flowers,
kind words, and kind deeds.
-LONGFELLOW-
Friends are
the flowers in the
garden of life.

POST
WEEDS • WEEDS •

I think there are as many kinds of gardening as of poetry.

–JOSEPH ADDISON–

Scatter seeds of kindness
Everywhere you go;
Scatter bits of courtesy-
Watch them grow and grow.
Gather buds of friendship;
Keep them till full-blown;
You will find more happiness
Than you have ever known.

—Amy R. Raabe—

LOVE
HAPPINESS

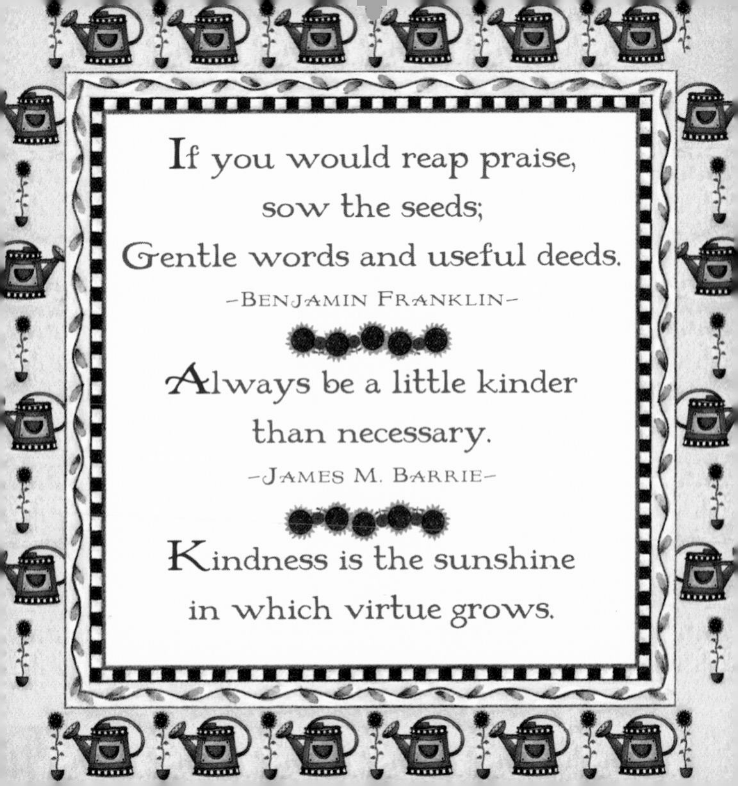
If you would reap praise,
sow the seeds;
Gentle words and useful deeds.
–Benjamin Franklin–
Always be a little kinder
than necessary.
–James M. Barrie–
Kindness is the sunshine
in which virtue grows.

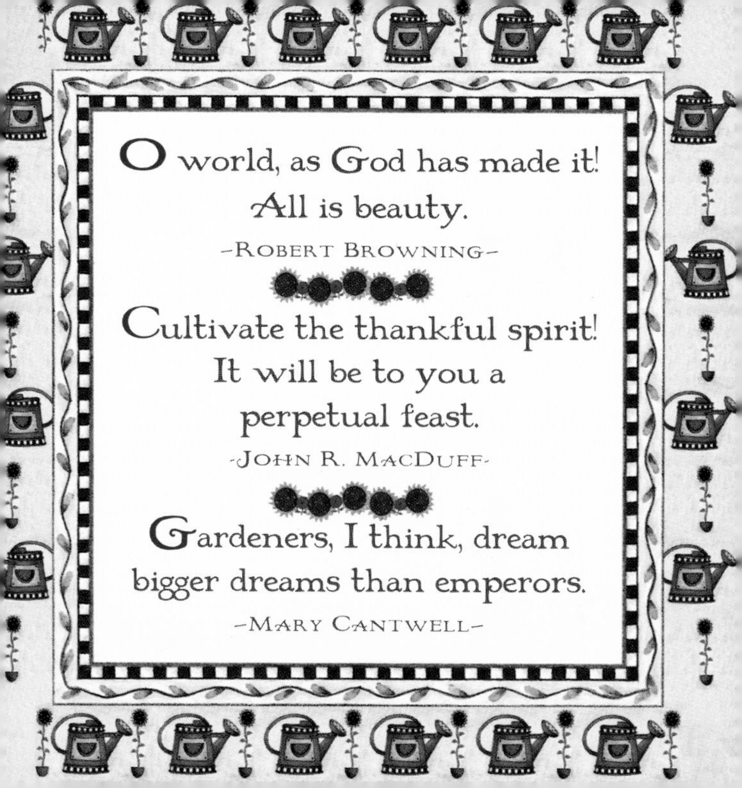
O world, as God has made it!
All is beauty.
–Robert Browning–
Cultivate the thankful spirit!
It will be to you a
perpetual feast.
-John R. MacDuff-
Gardeners, I think, dream
bigger dreams than emperors.
–Mary Cantwell–

All gardens are a form of autobiography.

–Robert Dash–

FEED & SEED
BIRD SEED MIX
©Debbie Mumm

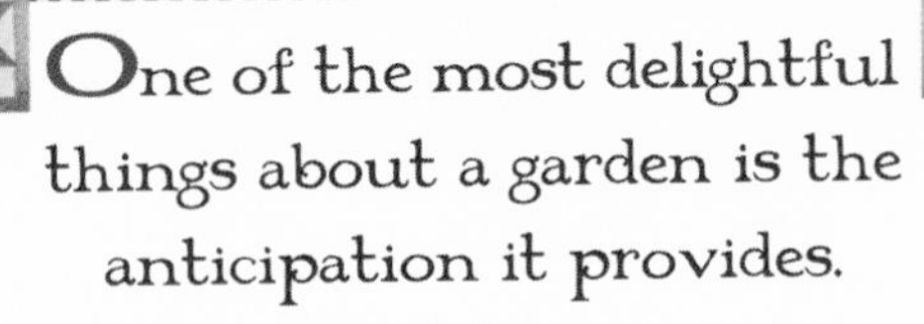

One of the most delightful things about a garden is the anticipation it provides.

–W. E. Johns–

O the green things growing,
the green things growing,
The faint sweet smell of
the green things growing!

–Dinah Mulock Craik–

DAISY

LOVE IS NOT ENOUGH
Love of flowers and vegetables
is not enough to make
a good gardener.
He must also hate weeds.
–EUGENE P. BERTIN–

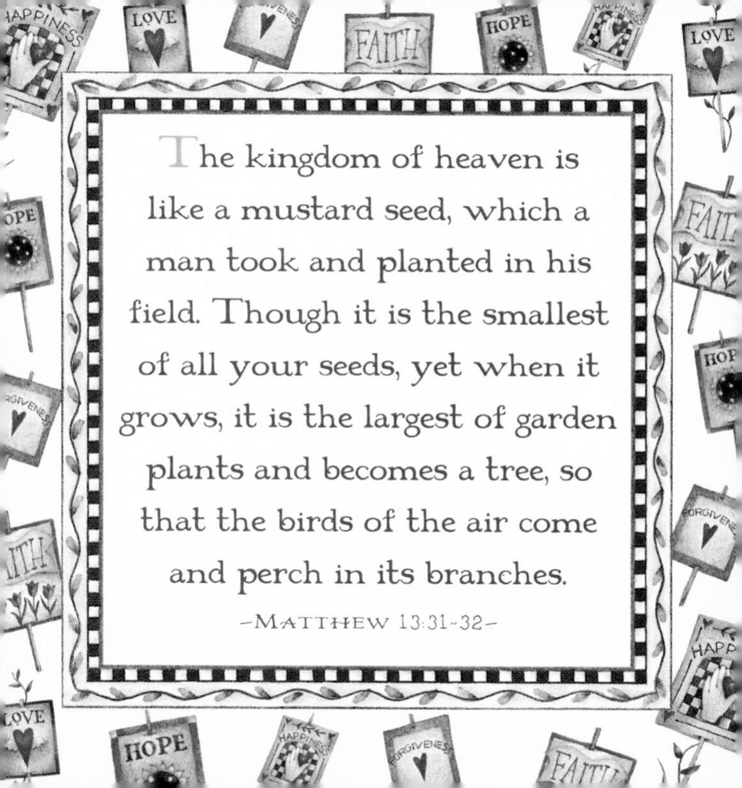

The kingdom of heaven is like a mustard seed, which a man took and planted in his field. Though it is the smallest of all your seeds, yet when it grows, it is the largest of garden plants and becomes a tree, so that the birds of the air come and perch in its branches.

–MATTHEW 13:31-32–

PERFECT
WEEDS

Adam was gardener, and God,
who made him, sees that
half of all good gardening is
done upon the knees.

–Rudyard Kipling–

The smallest seed of faith
is better than the largest
fruit of happiness.

–Henry David Thoreau–

He who plants a garden
plants happiness.

–CHINESE PROVERB–

I wish everybody had a
garden, and would
work in it himself.
The world would grow
sweeter-tempered at once.

–ANNA WARNER–

Show me your garden and
I shall tell you what you are.

–ALFRED AUSTIN–

Sunflower Sylvia
He who plants a sunflower plants joy.
© DEBBIE MUMM

As you sow,
so shall ye
reap unless
of course
you are
an amateur
gardener.

forget me nots
©Debbie Mumm

©DEBBIE MUMM

To dig and delve in nice clean dirt
Can do a mortal little hurt

-John Kendrick Bangs-

No occupation is so delightful
to me as the culture of the earth.

-Thomas Jefferson-

I have never had so many good
ideas day after day as when I
work in the garden.

-John Erskine-

Like gardeners,
we need to learn that
we can't plant and
reap the same day.

GARDEN of PLENTY
HOPE
FAITH
LOVE
HAPPINESS
In the sweetness of Earth's Garden, Sow seeds of hope and love ♥ Nurture buds of growth ♥ Encourage strong roots ♥ Harvest rich abundance
GARDEN

Button-Eyed Annie

It takes a long time
to grow an old friend.

—John Leonard—

You who dwell in the gardens
with friends in attendance,
let me hear your voice!

—Song of Songs 8:13—

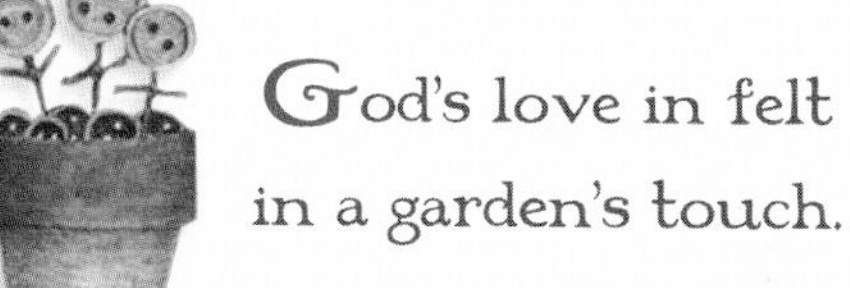

God's love in felt
in a garden's touch.

God Almighty first planted a garden; and indeed, it is the purest of human pleasures.

–FRANCIS BACON–

The most beautiful discovery true friends make is that they can grow separately without growing apart.

–ELISABETH FOLEY–

I like gardening but I have
a very modest garden.
I do a little, but not much,
they just grow.
It's a miracle,
the way God meant it.

–ELLEN GOODMAN–

What is paradise?
but a garden, an
orchard of trees
and herbs full of pleasure
and nothing there
but delights.

–William Lawson–

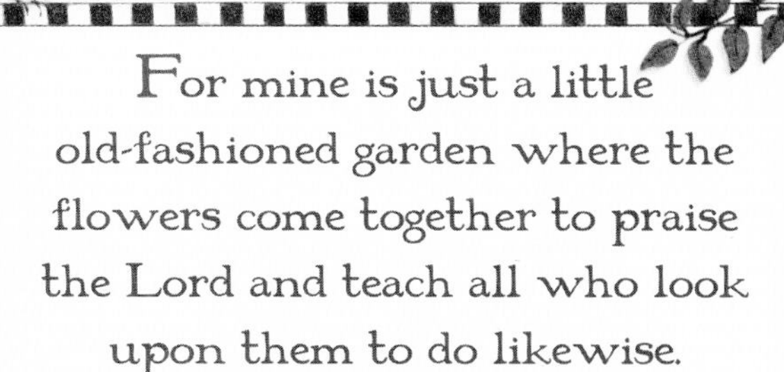

For mine is just a little old-fashioned garden where the flowers come together to praise the Lord and teach all who look upon them to do likewise.

—Celia Thaxter—

FEED & SEED
BIRD SEED MIX
©Debbie Mumm

I am the vine; you are the branches. If a man remains in Me and I in him, he will bear much fruit.

–JOHN 15:5–

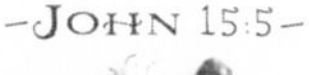

But a little garden, the littler the better, is your richest chance for happiness and success.

–REGINALD FARRER–

Old Roses
PERFECT
WEEDS
©Debbie Mumm

If you once loved a garden
that love will stay with you.

-Louise Driscoll-

Half the interest of a
garden is in the constant
exercise of imagination.

-Mrs. C. W. Earle-

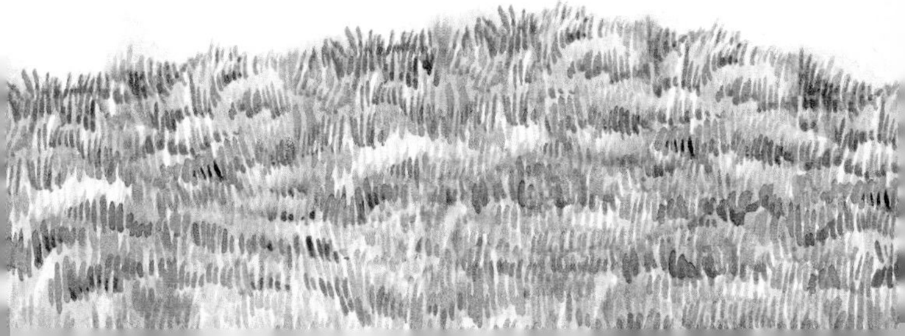

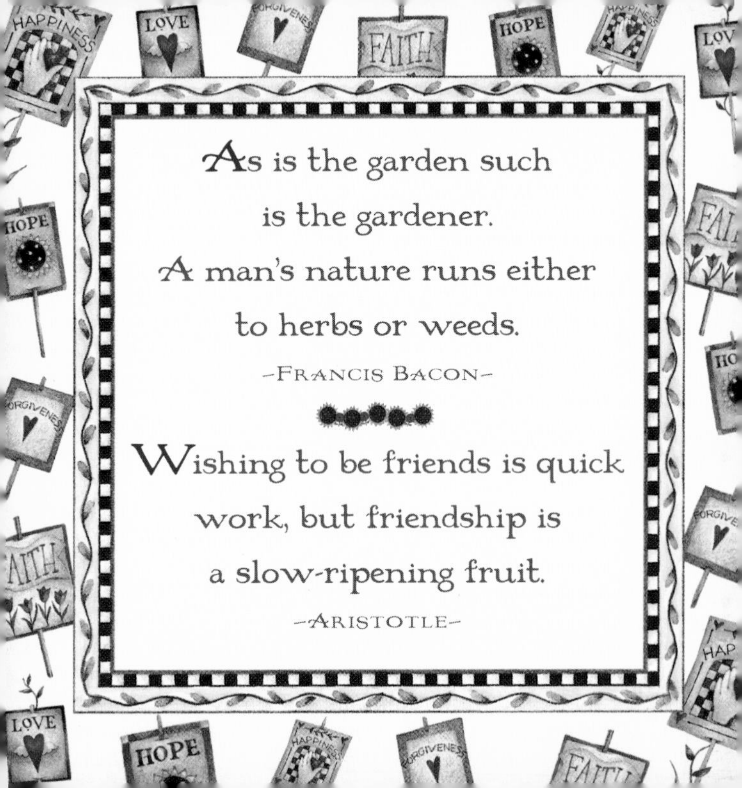

As is the garden such
is the gardener.
A man's nature runs either
to herbs or weeds.

—Francis Bacon—

Wishing to be friends is quick
work, but friendship is
a slow-ripening fruit.

—Aristotle—

One of the healthiest ways to gamble is with a spade and a package of garden seeds.

—Dan Bennett—

Like life, few gardens have only flowers.

Friendship is a plant which must often be watered.

—German Proverb—

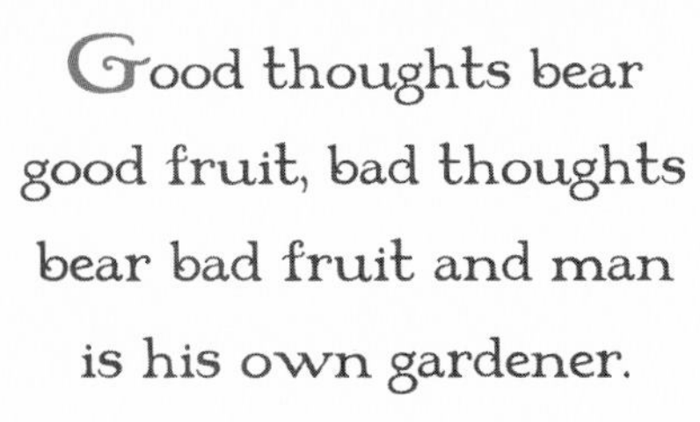

Good thoughts bear
good fruit, bad thoughts
bear bad fruit and man
is his own gardener.

–JAMES ALLEN–